I0232352

www.finishinglinepress.com

Repaired

poems by

Jenny A. Burkholder

Finishing Line Press
Georgetown, Kentucky

Repaired

ACKNOWLEDGMENTS

Thank you to the editors of the following journals for publishing my poems:

Emerge Literary Journal: Eve Dreaming
The Prose-Poem Project, an online and print journal sponsored by Equinox
Publishing, Shelburne, VT: Dorothy
Forward: Deconstructing the Right Breast
Spoon River Poetry Review: Mistranslation
Poemmemoirstory: New Year's Eve

Publisher: Leah Maines

Editor: Christen Kincaid

Cover Art: John D. Flak, www.flakphotography.com

Author Photo: John D. Flak, www.flakphotography.com

Cover Design: Elizabeth Maines

Printed in the USA on acid-free paper.
Order online: www.finishinglinepress.com
also available on amazon.com

Author inquiries and mail orders:
Finishing Line Press
P. O. Box 1626
Georgetown, Kentucky 40324
U. S. A.

Table of Contents

For John, Rainey, and Harper

New Year's Eve
Beebe, Arkansas 2011

Thousands of red-throated blackbirds
drop from the sky,
land with a thud against frozen
packed mud, on car hoods, and empty streets,
their imprints purpling the whole town.
Nobody notices.
Somewhere a helicopter hovers
over a car crash on a desolate
highway. Somewhere teens
kiss with sloppy tongues
in darkened closets.

It is a beginning and an end,
an Ouroboros. Like stones
they litter open fields.
Their red-blackness like
the curves of a throat.
For many the last day of the year
has the scent of lemons,
a divine prophecy:
you will be sent a boat
upon which you must sail.

Eve Dreaming

Tonight she practices Spanish, resting
her heavy limbs on a tiny metal chair
in a hotel café. *Acaba de llegar*
she says with an unusually fluent
tongue. Of course, she is naked, full of light.

Careful not to bump the small table
between them, Adam snaps a photograph
of their thimbles of tequila. Eve is in love
with smoking, letting her last
cigarette burn to empty between disintegrating fingers.
Tomorrow promises to be
a how-to on properly using a knife
and fork. Next week, horseback riding.
She knows, all too well, how to be an intrepid—
lessons etched like scars—yet wordless student.

Dorothy

In my red high heels, a Rolex with a face of a hundred tiny diamonds, and my new black leather dress snuggled around my hips, I plan to smoke three cigarettes. First one I'll light with a plastic Bic lighter, rough around the edges from opening too many beer tops, and inhale deeply. The sky, really the lid of a jigsaw puzzle box, breaks apart into two hundred and fifty pieces. I'm going to click my heels and sing. Not the song that you would think, though. Because I am feeling artsy, I'll call it "World Crumble." And as I am crossing and uncrossing my legs, checking the red spot above my knee, I may engage in some idle chitchat with a young skateboarder who sits next to me. His wallet dangles from a chain at his belt loop, and he wears a beat up T-shirt of some now defunct rock band. He's too young to smoke, but he plucks a cigarette out from behind my ear like a magician and lights it up for me. Who am I to say stop? I wistfully blow smoke down Kedzie Avenue, watching the old men of Humboldt Park disappear in its haze. These men, the sentries of this fairy tale, their worn grooves our sidewalk, guard my friend and me. We trade our own stories of bravery until it's past his curfew. This is when I light up my third cigarette. Everything is different when smoking your last; there's a finality and reassurance that the world is whole and beautiful, right like a flagpole. And I am different, more relaxed and watery, my own reflection heartening me.

Eve Reconsiders

They threw their dirt-bike insults,
so she wrapped her embarrassed body
in button ups and button downs
and hid behind a chrome-plated heart.

She wrapped her embarrassed body
in borrowed clothes and worn out pants
and hid a behind chrome-plated heart
at the bike rack behind school.

In borrowed clothes and worn platitudes
voices jangled in her like change
at the bike rack behind school,
their sturdy-chair like wisdom not something to sit on.

Her voice jangled in her ear like change
warning her to hide her rage.
The sturdy-chair like wisdom cracking
from the weight of a cocked fist.

Twin

You entered the front door of the world first, a struggling curve
and pond. To be born even a moment after means I am

now an empty rocking chair, standing on the crumbling balcony
of our childhood, memory emptying and filling

like a pail. There we are in the living room of our loneliness,
grandmother's paper cuttings, mismatched and scattered,

or in her shoe boxes angling our way into the mirror in green
spiky leather and black beaded dresses. Without you,

I am the backdoor where weary branches settle, where bells
ring out in hopes of shattering this frame we share.

This Is a Purple World

She presses her ear to the kitchen floor.
Thousands of miles away, war
simmers and steams. Here
to protect her species, her spine
a glowing purple rod of light,
skin a palette of white oak
bark, as brave as a magnolia's
triumphant white petals. Filled
with controlled fury, her fragrance
startles us all. Only six, she rides
her yellow banana handled bike,
stares with an unblinking elephant
eye, hears what we cannot:
a deep exhale, something like hope
crossing borders, seeping through
cracks in the tiles.

Saturday Night Fever

Worn blank face
of kitchen table
is an ever-widening
circle of desire,
a crowded discotheque
where John Travolta,
white wide pants,
blousy black shirt
and sheen collar,
sprayed open for his wildly
hairy chest, effortlessly hitch
kicks and splits the dance floor.
Mondrian of yellow, red
and blue flashing lights,
his radiance spins
in the mirror ball.

Work Area Ahead

Methodical *Beep Beep Beep*
of reverse, moving
backwards, receding.
Slumberous backhoe,
protruding head
and awkward talons
like an extinct dinosaur
in front of my neighbor's
FOR SALE sign.
Men and women in orange
reflective vests, yellow hard hats,
a prehistoric cadre dance the dance
of SLOW DOWN and STOP
with all that pass. Dump truck's mournful
yawl realizes its job is to
let go. Everywhere there's a hole
to be fixed and pageantry never ending.

Twenty-seven ways to put you back together

Needle and thread
patches and darning.
Crying, splint, cast, stucco.

Ignoring. A screwdriver.
Bribery. Extortion. Band aids or tourniquet.

Talk therapy. Rope. Wrench.
Antibiotics. Glue and tape.
Paint or salve. Putty.
Negation. Medication.
Metaphor. Hand cream.

Diagnosis

The Dead. The Disappeared. The Silent.
Visit me one night.

We ride the yellow school bus,
tall black seats dividing us. Cancer

is a one-way street moving only east.

The Disappeared's long red fingernails
reach over to brush my left cheek.

No stop signs. No breaks.
The Dead smiles
his same smile as in life.

Wide white teeth, fresh stubble
covering his neck and chin.

How long has it been since he soared
off the Golden Gate Bridge like a trumpeter

swan and landed in the icy Bay? In the driver's
long rearview mirror, he nods.

No longer do I need to worry
about the right shoes. *It doesn't matter.*

The Silent casually holds my hand
in her empty lap. Screeching brakes.
Honking horns. *It will all be fine.*

Deconstructing the Right Breast
(all italics from REPORT OF OPERATION 05/07/12)

The patient was taken to the operating room
reliving 10th grade,

how she chased warm gin with milk.

Following induction of general anesthesia, I marked
out a circumareolar incision on the right breast
like a treasure map
to perform the mastectomy and axillary dissection
through the area.

Both breasts, arms, axilla, and abdomen
beautiful, pink, exposed
were prepped and draped in a sterile

white papery *fashion*

We infiltrated, black construction paper sky, pinpricked
to let stars shine through *the right breast*
with local anesthetic, a double shot

for tumbling down
a flight of dark stairs. *A #15 blade*

was used to make a skin incision.

Decision. Collision. Admission. Glisten. Forgiven.

Flaps were raised

like Buddhist prayer flags, their sadhana of non-attachment

superiorly, medially, inferiorly, and laterally,
all with electrocautery.

Superiorly to the clavicle, those lovely hollows

medially shining the sun to the sternum,

inferiorly to the rectus abdominis, two canals of muscle

laterally a bridge to be crossed *to the latissimus.*

The breast was taken off

In its place: thrumming, an embroidery
of sunflowers, thistle, mist.

From Mud to Miracle

Freshly trimmed third green soaks
our flimsy t-shirts, cigarette smoke
unfolds like paper napkins.

Our exhales are warm but frail
as they hobble above us, knees

curve like the bridge we rode
our bikes under that day
along the tree-lined toe path
of the Erie Canal.

Our bodies are well-packed suitcases.

For your heart, black, open toed
strappy sandals. Mine
something in brown, sensible,
and thick-soled.

At one point on our journey,
we stopped for a cow
in a deserted muddy pasture.
Inside his salvaged, gray eyes
was a crisscrossed map of the sky.

Under this sky,
so close now it's hard to breathe,
love gives up and stars fall

leaving white trails
glistening within me.

(Title taken from a line in Richard Buckner's song titled "Mud" on
Bloomed)

Still Life, 1999

Outside my second floor window, an empty
lot unfurls Big Bluestem, flourishing
in the heat. Someone has pressed fast
forward on regeneration, lot
slowly mending itself and turning
back into tall grass prairie.

One day a couple moved there,
their conversations a beaten up mumble
of what couples keep between them.
They had a hairbrush and red bike.

I watched them, her chest a garden
of goldenrod and his, a carpet of blazing
stars, not to be held back or stopped.

Boxing up the trash of one's heart
is as natural as Indian grass shoving
its way up through forgotten concrete,

nature seeking the matted imprints
of their bodies, a reminder
of its own longing.

Women and Children First

When we kiss
        ocean surface,
land two miles before
        tarmac and when doors
open for us to escape
        cabin's flowering pressure,
we will be first. We will
        wave to you as we glide
down yellow inflatable
        slide into waiting
dinghy. You will stand
        at the door, helping others
like us—women and children—
        they, too, whispering goodbye.
The mouth is not big
        enough for your waving
hands. Our dinghy
        cannot hold all this sorrow,
and space between us
        continues to widen.
Opening like an envelope—
        we drift farther away.
My love,
        your boat
will be coming soon.

Swan

And then a murky gray June
dawn, sun winking its way
through the haze, Icarus, stretching
his fecund wings and soaring out across
a palette of luminous sky.

We know the rest, sun burnt waxwings.

Sinuous neck stretching forward.
It's a magnificent ending, sumptuous
and grand. That's the fairy tale.

Your soft body will not survive impact,
slapping the serene face of the Bay.

Once the fog limps its way out,
it's just orange rusty peaks
of the Golden Gate Bridge aching
up into the sky like bony knees.

Postcards

I.

Careening the wooden banister
down to your family below.
They could not read
your handwriting, letters scratched
with twigs into an inky
mess. They did not try.

II.

Crown of clover laces
your head. *I'm alive*
gets written with grasses
and leftover needles
until the rains come.

III.

All of this is against instinct.

IV.
Soon, home.
Soon, my love, I will be home.
My suitcase a red bird,
clothes a tangle of branches.
For you my love, snapshots:
the earth a rusty bolt,
skein of blue ice
swatch of yellow paint.

V.

Silent, scratched, and peeled,
sent to the wrong address.

Jean Genet Refuses a Shower

All italics taken from Jean Genet's The Thief's Journal

Stuffed with cotton like a rag doll
with black button eyes and yellow stretched

seams, his shirt twists at his waist.

Within his body *the sun rose, continued its curve*
and completed it.

Genet means broom.

Like a cockroach inching
its way out of the drain, he's dirty
with his own mythology— the *close relationship between flowers*
and convicts.
The fragility and delicacy of the former
are of the same nature as the brutal insensitivity of the latter.

A universe unfolds, *sparkling with all my gestures,*
within him, and his prisoner
stares back at him. *I know nothing of the mother*

who abandoned me in the cradle—
his goose winged heart flutters—
loneliness and despair of the traveler who has lost his shadow.

Hitchhiking

Botched wisdom. Maybe that's what got her into this mess, hustling across Athens on the back of some Greek guy named Milton's moped. When she asks if he has read *Paradise Lost,* he laughs, doesn't really get the joke, and wants her to run away with him and waitress in his nightclub. Corfu, that's where she's trying to get to, but all she hears in her head are her mother's forewarnings: "Eat your peas. It will keep you wise." Or "Forget it if they talk behind your back. They are just jealous." They speed across town. "Opposites attract. Looks are nothing," her mother preached, and she disobeyed. Quickly. Right now, she has just grabbed a ride with the best looking man to stop. "An apple a day keeps the doctor away," that voice traversing continents and firmly messing up her plans. Now, she's scared. "Up ahead, I see the ferry station. Right up ahead. Let me off," she screams into Milton's ear. Very abruptly he slams on the brakes and deposits her at the corner; he points towards the left and says, "Corfu." Wearily, she waves goodbye, promises to come visit his bar. She's ready to escape her mother's voice in her ear, the sticky feeling of his leather jacket on her arms, and when she turns the corner, she realizes they have gone in a large, tormented circle.

Mistranslation

My hairdresser can barely fix my crooked bangs.
Her pinky is in a makeshift splint.
In an argument, she punched
her ex, met some friends at the Rainbo,
stayed out all night, drinking.
This is not unusual—for her—
but today with new scissors poised
right above my eyebrow, her problems seem
specifically mine. These days full

of dread. Once, my mother explained
my "open face" and all I could imagine, at the time,
were two slices of orange cheddar melting
over whole-wheat toast. She tried
to explain the fallen, those who believe
in routine. Those who one day, day like any other,
hop in the car, and never get under
way. They hear the moon's shade humming
their tune. There are many of us—
translucent and spent. We choose
subtle pastels for bedroom walls, watch films
in just our underwear, take special care
of our skin. Yet mornings we peer out
over the playground, backyard, empty
lot, and realize even our sky
spills the white of ruin.

This Is Me Watching the Sky Watch the Beach

We spot you running towards us
like a Polaroid image coming

into focus. We don't have to commit here—

all expanse not expense,

a lesson in impermanence,
breathtaking beauty.

The ocean does what
it wants, rising and swelling beyond

its barriers onto
an infinitely erasable shore.

Additional Acknowledgements

Thank you to Western Michigan University, the Illinois Arts Council, the Vermont Studio Center, RopeWalk Writers Retreat, and the Postgraduate Writers' Conference at Vermont College of Fine Arts for supporting my work. Thank you to my poetry group: Mary Lynn, Jane, Jack, and David for writing, reading, and caring about poetry. Thank you to my fabulous friends and colleagues for supporting me. Thank you to all of my poetry and yoga teachers, their teachers, and their teachers' teachers. And most importantly, thank you to my family.

Jenny A. **Burkholder** currently teaches English at Abington Friends School, a Quaker co-educational school in Jenkintown, Pennsylvania. She lives with her photographer husband and two fairy-house-building daughters. She has a B.A. with Special Honors in English from The George Washington University, an M.F.A. from Western Michigan University, and an M.S. Ed. from Northwestern University. Her poems have been published in *New American Writing, The Spoon River Poetry Review, poemmemoirstory, Emerge Literary Journal, The Prose-Poem Project,* and *Glimmer Train.* Her creative nonfiction was recently published in the online issue of *So to Speak: A Feminist Journal of Language and Art.* She's received an Illinois Arts Council Fellowship for Poetry and won the *Glimmer Train* October Poetry Open. When she's not writing, she's practicing yoga and recently completed her yoga teacher training at Blue Banyan Yoga.